A WRITTEN PERSP

SOMERSET & DORSET RAILWAY

Tales from the footplate

Wallace Moon & Geoff Akers

&

Just like my dreams

John Bailey

First published in Great Britain in 2016 / 2019

© *John Bailey, 2025*

All Rights Reserved. No part of this publication may be reproduced, stored in a retrieval system, or transmitted in any form, or by any means, electronic, mechanical, photocopying, recording or otherwise without the prior permission in writing of the copyright holders, nor be otherwise circulated in any form or binding or cover other than in which it is published and without a similar condition being imposed on the subsequent publisher.

The illustrations used in this book are derived from original photographs in The Norman Lockett Archive, as supplied by and © copyright of David Lockett, who has asked that all reproduction fees/royalties be donated to the Somerset & Dorset Railway Heritage Trust.

Except:

Page 30 Illustration derived from an original photograph from Keith Barrett's Collection and remain © copyright Keith Barrett

Page 37 Illustrations derived from an original photograph from John Chalcroft and remain © copyright John Chalcroft who has asked that all reproduction fees/royalties be donated to the Somerset & Dorset Railway Heritage Trust

Page 42, 44 (a) Illustrations derived from original photographs by John Strange and remain © copyright Duncan Chandler Collection who has asked that all reproduction fees/royalties be donated to the Somerset & Dorset Railway Heritage Trust

ISBN: 9798289627766
Imprint: Independently published

TIME TO REMINISE

Growing up a young boy in Chilcompton I was privileged to live just 200 yards or so from the station. I can recall even now as if it was only yesterday the Somerset & Dorset Railway station at Chilcompton. I must have been about the age of five or six, but I remember the early evening train hurtling down the up line (that always confused me at the time) whistle blowing towards Bath at around 6.30 signalling it was time for bed.

I became a frequent visitor to the station to see the trains and can remember being in awe seeing Evening Star and to experience the Pines Express hurtling through, wondering why it never stopped at Chilcompton. Changes were coming but being so young I couldn't understand why suddenly the Pines Express was no longer running.

They say it was every boy's dream to be an engine driver and work on the railway, and I was no exception.

The years went by and bestowed warm-hearted memories of trips on the train. But at the age of nine something was happening, and I couldn't really understand what. Things were starting to look a little run down, then suddenly the adults are talking about the end of the train service, and it would have to be buses from now on. The date for closure was set for January 1966 and as it came around, I thought that was it. Then out of the blue I heard that it was not closing in January, and being just nine years old, thought we would be keeping our railway. I was told something about the buses not available to replace the trains.

Of course, my adulation was short lived as it turned out to be only a temporary reprieve. I can still recall sitting on the embankment at Chilcompton station just a couple of months later to wave a sad farewell to the last train to run over the Somerset & Dorset on 6th March 1966. The line closed the next day.

Could this be forever, I always hoped not, but as time went on the infrastructure began to be dismantled and the railway was gone.

A foreword by John Baxter

Page 6

PART ONE

Page 10

A journey on the Somerset & Dorset Railway from Bath Green Park to Bournemouth West accompanied by tales from the footplate

PART TWO

Page 87

Just like my dreams - a short story of a flight of fantasy on the Somerset & Dorset Railway circa 1985

FOREWORD

On my 13th birthday on March 28th, 1963, I travelled from Trowbridge to Bath Spa, then walked to Bath Green Park to catch a train from that station for the first time. I had 7/6d (37½p) on me which, in retrospect, would probably have got me a return ticket to Templecombe.

However, I had only started trainspotting in 1961, and my locomotive mecca was nearby Westbury, a short 1-shilling (5p) train journey away. Train journeys with mates were restricted to what we could afford and for me that was how many weddings took place at Holy Trinity where they wanted a choir which provided me with 2/6d (12½p) on each occasion. In the school holidays it was Wednesdays at Swindon Works and if I could afford it on my additional weekly pocket money Bristol Temple Meads. I'd seen the last Pines' thunderous exit southwards at the hands I found years later of Peter Guy and Ron Hyde and I bunked 82F on more than one occasion as I recently found a list of all the engines I had cabbed over the years.

Despite all this, incredulously I hadn't any knowledge of the Somerset & Dorset or its delightful stations and I had no idea that, at Bath Green Park, one of the most delightful lines in the country veered off to the left at Bath Junction. And so, when I arrived at the Bath Green Park ticket office I asked for a return from Bath to Bristol TM via Bitton and Mangotsfield and didn't even bother to take notice of some of the other destinations such as Radstock and Midsomer Norton on the finger boards. All I remember of that journey was that it was a Standard tank with 3 coaches and that it wasn't all that heavily loaded, that day being a Thursday. So, the one opportunity I had to travel over the whole of the northern section of the S&D had gone and within just a few years Beeching and Barbara Castle had done their worst.

It was the Reverend Alan Newman (who had officiated at my marriage to Mary Anne in 1975) who introduced me to Ivo Peters, and it was his photos that really started my interest in the S&D and my eternal regret that I never travelled over its length. An inspirational man, his private showings of his wonderful films at his home in The Circus and his erudite commentary had me hooked. Eventually that resulted in an association with the S&D via

Washford and Midsomer Norton station that continues to this day.

Whilst I had, in the late 70s, walked the line where I could from Bournemouth West to Bath Green Park my aim was always to help re-open a section of the line to steam. The commemorations for March 2016 on the 50th anniversary of the line's closure brings that aim to fruition. There have been many S&D events on other larger preserved railways, and these will no doubt continue, but do remember that nothing will ever compare with a trip behind steam over the real S&D.

It is somewhat ironic that the signatory on the railways notice of closure, Barbara Castle's Parliamentary Under-Secretary was one J. Baxter and that another J. Baxter has worked tirelessly with many others to reverse a part of that fateful decision. He of course was doing as he was told by his political masters, but I don't have those same constraints!

We intend to go from strength to strength and the commemorations for 2016 will provide a catalyst for both consolidation and future extension. When we all can drive and fire a 7F at Midsomer Norton, my 40-year personal and financial journey will all have been worth it.

So do enjoy John's fine book whilst you also enjoy the "Family Line" and real S&D at Midsomer Norton now and in the future.

John Baxter

Secretary to Somerset & Dorset Railway Heritage Trust 2016

BATH GREEN PARK
via Templecombe to
BOURNEMOUTH WEST

Ticket in hand, sandwiches packed, so sit back and enjoy a journey with me on the Somerset & Dorset Railway. From Bath Green Park we travel south to Bournemouth West on a stopping train. The journey is enhanced with annotations from the footplate from Geoff Akers (GA) and Wallace Moon (WM).

Departure 8.30am

DISTANCE TO BOURNEMOUTH 71½ Miles

The station here at Bath Green Park was originally opened in 1870, at that time known as Queens Square, to serve the extension from Bristol to Bath for the Midland Railway. The station facade was built in a style to blend with the buildings in the Georgian City with a vaulted glass roof covering the single span wrought iron structure.

The glass roof protects part of the two platforms from the elements with the south platform normally used for departures. The two siding between allow arriving locomotive to run back to the turntable to prepare for the outward journey. The turntable, locomotive sheds and goods yard are about half a mile from the terminal building.

Upon completion of the Somerset & Dorset extension in 1874 the connection was made by means of a new Midland Bridge close to the locomotive sheds. This paved the way for through trains from the Midlands to the South Coast. The through trains reverse here at Bath including the Pines Express from Manchester to Bournemouth West.

BR Standard Class 5 4-6-0 No. 73050 awaiting departure to Bournemouth

On normal weekdays the station is relatively quiet for a terminal in stark contrast to summer Saturdays when the station becomes very busy with holiday trains from the north to Bournemouth. The Pines Express service was introduced in 1910 and still runs daily from Manchester to Bournemouth. The Pines Express is often double headed due to the gradient between Radstock and Maesbury.

Within the elegant facade are the Booking Office, Parcels Office, Refreshment Rooms, Ladies and Gentleman's Waiting Rooms and the offices of the S&DJR. A delightful setting to begin the journey to Bournemouth.

BR Class 9F 922220 Evening Star waiting to depart from Bath Green Park

FROM THE FOOTPLATE

GA

Before the train can get underway from Bath Green Park we must carry out what is called a preparation link. The driver and fireman prepare the engine to go out into traffic for when the driver and fireman who are going to work that train come on duty a half an hour before it is due to leave the loco shed.

We prepare the fire by laying the fire up, ensure that the lamps are on the engine and that the sand boxes are full. We have to check that the fire irons are on the back of the tender, check that we have a coal shovel and a peck on the engine and make sure the engine is nicely swilled down and tidy for the driver and fireman to come on the engine and take it out into traffic.

We also have a disposal link for when the driver and fireman return an engine to Bath Green Park. They must turn the engine and run it back to the locomotive shed over the pit. They both leave the engine and that is the end of their shift. At this point another fireman and driver take over, drop the fire, coal the engine and replenish the water before the engine is put back in the shed for another day's journey.

LOCOMOTIVE SHEDS

The four road Somerset & Dorset Motive Power Depot at Bath is located about ½ a mile to the west of Bath Green Park Station in a wooden structure. The substantial shed is 300ft long and 60ft wide and can accommodate up to 18 locomotives.

The coal stage road is alongside with the turntable located adjacent. The 60ft turntable is shared between the Somerset & Dorset and the Midland shed. The two road Midland shed is a more robust structure built of stone and of course predates the Somerset & Dorset shed.

Today the shed is mainly used for major repairs and maintenance with the larger S&D shed used as the running shed. The current 60ft turntable, installed in 1934, replaced a smaller model. An extensive goods yard is located south of the sheds with a large goods shed, coal yard, and a grain depot.

There are several private sidings here at Bath including Bath Gas Works, Stothert & Pitt and the LMS Railway Company.

BATH JUNCTION

At Bath Junction we leave the Midland Line, now travelling on the Somerset & Dorset Railway extension over the Mendips to Evercreech junction. Bath Junction marks the start of a 1.50 climb for the next 2 miles to Combe Down tunnel. Bank engines are provided (Uncoupled) to assist freight trains as far as Combe Down tunnel.

The line from Bath Junction to Midford remains single track. All down trains must pick up a tablet. Most of the regular locomotives are equipped with a mechanical tablet catcher but if not, the fireman picks up the tablet by hand.

BR Class 5 No. 73012 joins the Midland line at Bath Junction

FROM THE FOOTPLATE

GA

Setting off from Bath Green Park every journey is different. It all depends on how the engine is going to behave. Many issues affect the performance, including what type of coal we have, how the driver has warmed the engine, and of course the fireman, and how good he is. Another important factor is how many carriages or wagons we have, and all these things will determine if we are going to have a good time heading up the 1.50 gradient towards Combe Down Tunnel, or whether it is going to be hard work.

DEVONSHIRE TUNNEL

FROM BATH GREEN PARK 2 Miles

DISTANCE TO BOURNEMOUTH 69½ Miles

As the train starts the climb out of Bath the first of the tunnels excavated for the Evercreech to Bath extension is encountered. Over a quarter of a mile long and with no ventilation Devonshire Tunnel is on a 1.50 gradient with the down train emerging below the northern slopes of Combe Down. The tunnel is named after Devonshire Buildings which are situated directly above.

FROM THE FOOTPLATE

GA

On reaching Devonshire Tunnel I can honestly say that if anyone has been to hell and back then they know what it is like in there for the crew on the footplate.

Going through the tunnel we have to get down on our hands and knees with a wet cloth over our face and we literally gasp for breath. The bore on Devonshire Tunnel is so small that one can sit on the driving seat or the fireman's seat with you elbow out the window and you can touch the side of the tunnel, it really is a confined space.

There is only 9 inches clearance between the top of the chimney and the roof of the tunnel. With the train developing over two thousand horsepower at the cylinder head it becomes extremely hot.

The conditions on the footplate are one of intense heat, smoke and sulphur fumes. The blast out of the chimney is so great that we sometimes blow the red bricks out of the roof. The intense heat from the chimney can melt the cement around the bricks and over time some do fall out, sometimes onto the engine or the tender, and occasionally onto the carriages.

When we emerge from Devonshire Tunnel into Lyncome Vale we are literally gasping for breath. If the un-thinkable would happen and the engine slip in the tunnel on the extreme 1.50 gradient we would have literally 2 minutes to say our prayers to our maker and would then probably meet him.

WM

The tunnels on the Somerset & Dorset were built at a time when locomotives were much smaller. Both Devonshire and Combe Down tunnels are killers especially on a busy Saturday during summer services.

On a lighter note, we rely on the station staff back at Bath Green Park to boil the kettle to fill our tea can as the water from the engine contains chemicals for water softening, so is not suitable for drinking. The tea is an essential part of our breakfast on the footplate which is cooked in seconds on the fireman's shovel.

On one occasion a driver placed his cooked breakfast on the reversing rack to eat after cooking it on the fireman's shovel. The shovel was disturbed by the vibration of a passing train and the eggs, bacon, fried bread and mushrooms all slid off the shovel onto the track. Mostly we toast cheese sandwiches on a toasting fork stored in the cab under the driver's jacket.

The Combe Down and Devonshire tunnels, along with the steep approach to Bath, are the primary reasons for maintaining a single track on this section of the Somerset and Dorset Railway, known as the Bath extension. Once through the Combe Down tunnel, the gradient decreases to primarily 1:100 towards Midford Station.

BR Class 5 No.73049 and SR Pacific No. 34043 Combe Martin emerge from Devonshire Tunnel coasting towards Bath.

COMBE DOWN TUNNEL

FROM BATH GREEN PARK 2½ Miles

DISTANCE TO BOURNEMOUTH 69 Miles

The tunnel has no ventilation along the entire 1,862-yard length, and at the time of construction was the longest un-ventilated tunnel in Britain.

Over time the lack of ventilation has caused problems to slow moving trains. During November 1929 the driver and fireman of a northbound goods train were overcome by smoke. The train was moving very slowly in the tunnel due to a heavy load starting from a standstill at Midford Station. The train ran away, crashing into the goods yard on the approach to Bath Green Park killing the driver and two railway employees in the yard.

MIDFORD 8.40am

FROM BATH GREEN PARK 4¼ Miles

DISTANCE TO BOURNEMOUTH 67¼ Miles

Midford station is unique being the only station on the Bath extension of the S&D to have wooden buildings. The station is built in an attractive setting with just a single platform on upside of the line built on a ledge along the hillside. Just north of the station the line runs under a minor road bridge known as The Long Arch which is 37 yards long due to being built on an angle.

There is a small goods yard located north of the station with two sidings. Immediately south of the station the line becomes double track as it crosses the viaduct which carries it across the main road, Midford Brook and the GWR's Limpley Stoke to Camerton branch line. The viaduct is supported by eight brick and masonry arches and is 168 yards in length.

The tablet collected at Bath junction is released at Midford to show that the single line section covered is now clear.

WHITAKER EXCHANGE APPERATUS

Somerset & Dorset locomotive engineer Alfred Whitaker has developed a mechanical device, part of which is attached to a locomotive cab, which catches a loop on a pouch containing a tablet. It is given up by the train at the end of the single line section being caught by a catcher fixed adjacent to the track.

The system has enabled the tablet to be exchanged at speeds of 40mph or more, thus speeding up trains through the single line working. As we leave Midford Station behind the views open up as crossing the Midford Viaduct onto the double track. The journey continues through the beautiful undulating Somerset countryside with the track making a series of reverse curves through the pleasantly wooded and pastoral Midford and Wellow Valleys.

SOMERSET COAL

The Somerset coalfields form part of a larger coalfield that stretches from southern Gloucestershire to the Mendip Hills covering an area of almost 240 square miles. A scheme was proposed in 1766 to connect the coalfields by means of a canal and in 1794 a committee was formed to construct the Somerset Coal Canal.

The Somerset Coal Canal was built as a narrow construction and completed in circa 1800. The canal connected Paulton and Timsbury to Camerton with two aqueducts at Dunkerton. The canal continued passing through Midford, Monkton Combe and Limpley Stoke before joining the Kennet and Avon canal. Plans for a southern canal never came to fruition with a horse drawn tramway laid along what would have been the towpath as an alternative. The route from Radstock to Midford with a tunnel at Wellow was eventually purchased in 1871 by the Somerset & Dorset Joint Railway for the proposed track bed.

The coming of the railways soon diverted coal from the canals leading to their rapid decline.

WELLOW 8.47am

FROM BATH GREEN PARK 6¾ Miles

DISTANCE TO BOURNEMOUTH 64¾ Miles

This picturesque small station situated close to the village is well used, partly since the local bus service is restricted to only one day a week.

Unlike Midford the station here at Wellow follows the tradition of the Somerset & Dorset Railway, built of limestone with a slate roof. There is a Station Master's Office and Booking Hall which also doubles as the Waiting Room. The signal box is located at the eastern end of the down platform.

SHOSCOMBE

AND SINGLE HILL HALT 8.52am

FROM BATH GREEN PARK 8½ Miles

DISTANCE TO BOURNEMOUTH 63 Miles

The halt for Shoscombe and Single Hill wasn't opened until September 1929, some 55 years after the completion of the Bath Extension. The two bare platforms afford no shelter from the elements but there is a small Ticket Office and Waiting Room at the end of the down platform.

The halt is very well used as roads to the village are extremely narrow.

Continuing south from Shoscombe and Single Hill Halt the countryside changes as we pass through Shoscombe Vale and nearby Foxcote before entering the Somerset Coalfields where sidings connect Writhlington and Braysdown Collieries before reaching the market town of Radstock.

THE RADSTOCK RAIL ACCIDENT

The 7th August 1876 was a Bank Holiday weekend, and the Somerset & Dorset Railway ran seventeen extra trains to cater for people enjoying the day off work. They were all taking advantage of the recent 1874 single line extension linking Bath and Bournemouth. Arrangements were made to decide which trains were to be delayed allowing the special trains to pass over the single line sections, but poor telegraph communications hampered this work throughout the day.

Two trains crashed head on near the Foxcote signal box at 11.20pm on the single stretch of track resulting in 15 deaths and several serious injuries. Both trains involved in the accident were unscheduled.

The down train was originally scheduled as an empty stock train but had passengers on board returning from a regatta at Saltford near Bath. The up train from Bournemouth had been hastily arranged because the scheduled train was overcrowded.

The conclusion was given that the underlying cause was that the Somerset and Dorset Railway was essentially bankrupt at the time of the crash.

This left the infrastructure inadequate to the demands of the traffic, and the staff were inadequately trained for their duties. Improvements on the section of track between Radstock and Wellow were soon implemented because of the accident with the track being doubled and staffing arrangements revised.

Radstock North. *Jinty 0-6-0T No. 47557 waiting to provide banking assistance to a freight train as far as Masbury summit*

RADSOCK NORTH 8.56am

FROM BATH GREEN PARK 10½ Miles

DISTANCE TO BOURNEMOUTH 61 Miles

Radstock North lies adjacent to the GWR's Radstock South station although the two are not connected. The train passes the extensive sidings and sheds known as Radstock Yard before reaching the station. A motive Power Depot houses locomotives used for shunting and banking duties. Banking engines are required for most freight trains over the gruelling 7½ miles to Masbury summit with much of the route having a 1.50 gradient. The yard provides private sidings for Writhlington and Braysdown collieries, Tyning and Middle Pit, Radstock Co-operative Bakery and a Wagon Works.

The station buildings built of limestone with a slate roof house the Booking Office and Waiting Room and are located on the up platform with a basic wooden shelter on the down platform. A footbridge provides a safe walkway between the up and down platforms.

THE CLIMB OVER THE MENDIP HILLS

Ahead of the climb the first level crossing on the line from Bath crosses the busy A367 road causing long tailbacks at busy periods, and lengthy delays in high summer. It really is quicker by train.

The relentless climb begins directly at 1.50 and in half a mile the line swings to the southwest crossing the GWR at the Five Arches, although the official title is the North Somerset Viaduct.

With the crossing gates closed BR Standard Class 5 4-6-0s Nos. 73047 and 73054 meet outside the signal box at the west end of Radstock North with the Bournemouth and Bath trains respectively

FROM THE FOOTPLATE

WM

The relatively easy section where we have coasted down from Midford allows the crew a respite and some time to admire the scenery. The Midford Valley always looks beautiful, especially with a profusion of primroses during the springtime.

Radstock is the first busy station out from Bath, particularly on market days. Through trains like the Pines Express are restricted to 40mph through the station. The climb will begin in earnest once we leave Radstock station and pass over the level crossing controlling the busy A367 road from Bath.

We now must ensure that we have a good bright fire to start the 1.50 gradient as we climb to cross the GWR line from Bristol in just ¾ of mile at the Five Arches.

GA

When working a twelve-coach excursion from Bristol to Bournemouth we must make sure when we arrive at Radstock to stop clear of the crossing, and not on it, to avoid holding up the traffic.

The Saturday excursions form Bristol to Bournemouth always stop at Radstock. We must be very careful when we pull away from the station because if we have too much water in the boiler the engine will prime, and we will have water going into the cylinders and coming out of the chimney.

Next to the station is the market hall which holds the popular Saturday market so if the engine is priming it chucks all the smoke box char bits out through the chimney, in that direction. The ladies walking around near the market in their nice white clothes would soon end up covered in black specks from the engine and this will then present British Railways with quite a large bill for cleaning.

MIDSOMER NORTON
SOUTH 9.05am

FROM BATH GREEN PARK 12½ Miles

DISTANCE TO BOURNEMOUTH 59 Miles

Two miles on a gruelling 1.50 ascent has brought us to Midsomer Norton South Station set high above the town located in the valley below. The gradient eases through the station to 1.300 but immediately at the end of the down platform increases again to 1.53 towards Chilcompton Tunnel.

Upon arrival at Midsomer Norton, the well-kept station and cultivated gardens are immediately noticeable. It is especially pleasing in the summer. Gracious rivalry exists between the Somerset & Dorset stations for the time-honoured 'Best Kept Station' award and here at Midsomer Norton they continue to win year after year. The award helped in no small way by the glorious floral displays.

The station building is in the customary style of the Somerset & Dorset Railway, built of limestone under a slate roof, and are located here on the down platform. The traditional stone buildings house the Station Masters Office, a Booking Hall, Booking Office and a Ladies Waiting Room.

A small wooden shelter provided respite from the elements on the up platform. The attractive signal box located on the up platform stands alongside the extremely well-tended garden and often frequented greenhouse. The traditional 'Sleeper' crossing between platforms for passengers is situated at the east end of the station, unlike the footbridge provided at Radstock.

The attractive signal box located on the up platform stands alongside the extremely well-tended garden

There are two short siding on the south side leading to a large goods shed. Shortly before the station we passed the siding giving access to the industrious Norton Hill Colliery. The National Coal Board (NCB) have their own locomotives used for shunting duties.

THE MENDIP HILLS

In 1870 plans were put forward by the Somerset & Dorset Railway to build an extension from the existing line at Evercreech Junction over the Mendip Hills to Bath. The construction was by no means an easy task, as the route would have to follow the contours of the hills to climb above 800ft to the summit of Maesbury (spelt Masbury by the railway), with many twists and turns along the way. Once completed it created a link from the Midlands via Bath to the south coast.

Numerous rock cuttings, embankments, tunnels and bridges had to be created along the 26-mile route. Work began in 1872, with the first passenger service commencing in July 1874.

FROM THE FOOTPLATE

WM

Midsomer Norton is an excellent station with their well-kept buildings and gardens. They have been prize winners on many occasions and all the staff contribute towards winning the award.

There is a permanent restriction through the station of 20mph for non-stopping trains because of the Silver Street Bridge.

There is also as section on the line with a 15mph restriction, due to a slip on the embankment which must be repacked with gravel twice daily, as the ballast is washed away by a hillside spring.

Radstock enginemen convey coal from Norton Hill colliery usually in 20 21T wagons to Evercreech Junction returning empty up the 1.50 gradient to Shepton Mallet back to Midsomer Norton.

Leaving the station is very hard work as the steep climb continues at the end of the platform and now continues all the way to Masbury summit.

As a fireman I must respond to a drivers request, and on one occasion was asked to bring my sandwich box to pick mushrooms he had spotted about 60 yards from the track. It however proved fruitless as they were pieces of limestone disturbed by the farmer's plough.

Class 7F 2-8-0 No 53808 passing Midsomer Norton with the Nottingham to Bournemouth (Saturday only) service.

The primary difficulty on the planned Bath extension from Evercreech Junction is now upon us. As we leave behind the brief respite of 1.300 at Midsomer Norton the gradient continues at a relentless 1.53 for most of the next 7 miles. The route follows the contours of the hillside out of Midsomer Norton but ¾ of a mile short of Chilcompton the line had to overcome a bluff in the hillside and the third significant tunnel on the route from Bath is soon encountered.

CHILCOMPTON TUNNEL

FROM BATH GREEN PARK 13¾ Miles

DISTANCE TO BOURNEMOUTH 57¾ Miles

Chilcompton Tunnel lies almost a mile north from Chilcompton Station. With the distinctive double bore the tunnel is a permanent reminder that the Somerset & Dorset 'Bath Extension' was originally built as a single line when opened in 1874. The doubling of the line between Radstock and Binegar was completed in 1886. The 66-yard-long tunnel is on a relentless 1.53 gradient and Locomotives emerging from the tunnel on the down road create an exhilarating sight and sound. Continuing south the Redan Curve offers a splendid view to the old part of the village of Chilcompton set in a quintessential Mendip valley.

FROM THE FOOTPLATE

GA

If the engine is behaving itself when we get to Midsomer Norton then we know we will have no problems going up the bank to Chilcompton, Binegar and over Masbury. Equally if the engine is playing up then we know we are going to have problems all the way up the bank to the summit. If the latter is the case, then we have the large fire irons out of the tender on the footplate ready to get the irons into the firebox to start moving the fire around.

The crew on the footplate have to be in charge of the engine not the other way around.

S&D Class 7F No 53807 approaching Chilcompton rock cutting. The extent of the Redan Curve is highlighted with the twin portals of Chilcompton Tunnel in the background

Previous image: Double Header Class 2P 4-4-0 No 40569 and BR Class 5 4-6-0 emerge from the original bore while the up line was not opened until 1886

CHILCOMPTON 9.14am

FROM BATH GREEN PARK 14½ Miles

DISTANCE TO BOURNEMOUTH 57 Miles

The gradient approaching from the rock cutting is a sever 1.50 for a short distance before briefly easing to 1.300 through the station.

The station here at Chilcompton was opened on 20 July 1874. There is a small goods yard with adjacent goods sheds and a large water tower dominating the neat station buildings. The platforms afford splendid views from their setting on the hillside above the valley. The main station buildings are situated on the down platform and are built in the traditional Somerset & Dorset style with a small wooden shelter on the exposed-up platform. The limestone building houses the Station Masters Office, Booking Hall and Ladies and Gentleman's Waiting Rooms.

A siding on the south side of the station is used for coal brought by road from the nearby New Rock Colliery. The station has a 5 Ton hand crane. Watercress grown in the valley below the station is transported by train to speed delivery for onward transportation to London and overseas. Two water columns, one on the up and one on the down line, are insulated to provide protection from Mendip winters.

Specially chartered trains from London arrive at the station for the beginning and end of each school term to cater for pupils who attend the nearby Downside School. As the train pulls away the brief respite of 1.300 through the station is replaced once again with the relentless climb.

BR standard Class 5 4-6-0 No 73052 arrives at Chilcompton with a southbound service Wood from Sheppard's timber yard in the background is transported by the railway

FROM THE FOOTPLATE

WM

The staff here at Chilcompton are well known to the crew on the footplate. Watercress is loaded onto the passenger train at the station but only for the good of the staff. We take on water at Chilcompton and in the winter this is a very cold and exposed spot, and we inevitably end up very wet. On the up line there is a permanent whistle board to warn workers in the deep cutting north of the tunnels.

The date was November 20th, 1950, and as we were passing Chilcompton signal box with a freight train on engine 13809, later re-numbered 53809, when signalman Bill Coombes held up a board on which was written 'IT'S A BOY'. My driver on this day was Horace (Nobby) Clark who could not believe I had come to work when my wife was expecting to give birth. I told him I could not afford to stay home as I had just been demobbed from the wartime Royal Navy and was in receipt of only a small sum from my 3 years' service as a telegrapher, having sailed around the world. Incidentally my captains name was Drake, Kenneth not Francis. Occasionally I have taken my son Richard on short trips on the footplate, but best to keep that quiet.

BR Class 4 2-6-0 No. 76006 departs Chilcompton for Bath

S&D Class 7F with freight from Evercreech Junction to Bath

Between Chilcompton and Binegar the line crosses the busy A37 and several other minor roads

FROM THE FOOTPLATE

WM

Still climbing the firemen works hard constantly supplying small amounts of coal all around the firebox every one or two minutes. During the coal shortage of 1945-1950 we were supplied with 'briquettes', a mixture of coal and cement in the shape of concrete blocks. These were later replaced with tennis ball shaped ones which rolled around on the floor of the cab.

LMS Class 4F 0-6-0 No 44422 with a stopping train from Bath to Templecombe

BINEGAR 9.22am

FROM BATH GREEN PARK 17 Miles

DISTANCE TO BOURNEMOUTH 54½ Miles

From Chilcompton the climb towards Masbury summit is relentless, however at Moorewood sidings the gradient eases slightly. The sidings at Moorewood are used by the Mendip Stone works at Emborough.

The station at Binegar serves the village and nearby Gurney Slade. The main building is situated on the up platform in contrast to the previous stations at Midsomer Norton and Chilcompton. The traditional Somerset & Dorset station houses the Station Masters Office, Booking Hall and Office and both a Ladies and Gentleman's Waiting Room. The signalman's house is adjacent to the station. The attached signal box and shelter are situated on the down platform opposite the main buildings.

Several sidings gain access to goods sheds and cattle loading pen. The early evening weekday service that runs from Bath terminates here at Binegar.

FROM THE FOOTPLATE

WM

The staff on the Somerset & Dorset are a very friendly bunch and none more so than here at Binegar. The Station Master, Norman Down, is always available to help when any problems arise, particularly during the Friday holiday train period. Winter can be harsh on Mendip with 1947 a particularly sever time.

Banking duties require a banking engine to assist by pushing freight trains from Radstock up the bank through Binegar as far as Masbury summit, just a mile or so on from Binegar station. We do this four times on one shift. My driver Aubrey Pearce is an excellent instructor tutoring me on both locomotives and first aid.

Aubrey's brother, Maurice, was fireman on engine No.13809 which was involved in the crash at Bath Junction ironically on 20th November 1929. Now re-

numbered 53809 every time we step on this engine Aubrey will say 20th November 1929 (recalling the accident). Maurice and his driver were overcome by fumes as water from the new engine leaked into the firebox. Henry Jennings, the driver, was killed in the runaway train collision and two other staff at Bath Yard.

A heavy fall of snow can transform the Mendip Hills into a winter wonderland but brings transport chaos to the roads and sometimes the railways. Winter on the Somerset & Dorset over the Mendip Hills can be in stark contrast to the lower lying track from Bath to Radstock and from Shepton Mallet to Templecombe. Snow can accumulate on the Mendip Hills while rain falls on the surrounding lower areas less than 300ft above sea level. The reason for the variation in weather is due to air temperature being reduced by 1 degree for every 330ft of elevation.

Binegar after a heavy snowfall, the snow having to be dug out before the plough engine could clear the line southwards

S&D Class 7F 53809 heading for Binegar to assist with problems caused by heavy snow falls on the Mendip Hills

MASBURY SUMMIT

The locomotive used to bank freight trains from Radstock can now drop off and return wrong track back to Binegar. The station is located about a ¼ mile south of the summit.

MASBURY HALT 9.26am

FROM BATH GREEN PARK 18¾ Miles

DISTANCE TO BOURNEMOUTH 52¾ Miles

We have now arrived at the remote Masbury Halt railway station, at 811 feet above sea level one of the highest in southern England. It opened on 20 July 1874 as Masbury but renamed Masbury Halt on 26 September 1938. The unmanned station serves East and South Horrington some 1½ and 2 miles distant.

Notwithstanding the remote location the platform on the up line has substantial stone buildings containing a Booking Office and Ladies and Gentlemen's Waiting Rooms. The station buildings are not in the traditional style of the Somerset & Dorset as there is no canopy. The signal box is also located on the up platform alongside the significant Station Masters House with an elaborate stone carving above a bay window. Shelter is provided for passengers on the down platform by means of a small wooden structure.

Magnificent views can be enjoyed south from nearby Maesbury Ring or Maesbury Castle, an Iron Age hill fort some 957 feet above sea level.

S&D Class 7F No 53807 nears the summit with the banker about to drop off

FROM THE FOOTPLATE

GA

At Masbury if the engine is playing up a bit and the water is down in the bottom of the gauge glass (The gauge glass measures the water level in the boiler to make sure you're making steam, but also operating safely with enough water to prevent any damage to the crown) with the engine now heading down the water will vanish to the front of the boiler.

If this were to happen, we are then in danger of melting the fusible plug in the crown of the firebox. Now if that lead plug melts, and there are two, one at the back and one in the front, it will let the water out of the boiler onto the fire to put it out, and we then have what is known as a failure. It is a safety procedure to prevent the firebox overheating and warping.

We have had a few near misses with both injectors on going downhill (The water injectors inject water from the tender into the boiler) not seeing the water come bobbing up in the gauge glass until we got down as far as Shepton Mallett and levelled out going over the viaduct.

As the line descends from the Mendip Hills towards Shepton Mallet it passes the fourth significant tunnel on the line at Windsor Hill. 1½ miles south of Masbury the corresponding lines pass through two separate tunnels.

The down line uses the old tunnel which is 239 yards in length being the original tunnel when the track operated as a single line. The up line uses the new tunnel which is only 126 yards long and was opened in 1892 when the line was doubled. North of the tunnels are the extensive sidings to Hamwood and Windsor Hill quarries. A stone-built signal box, as opposed to the traditional stone and wooden Somerset & Dorset stalwarts, was completed in 1892 when the line was doubled.

An unidentified BR Class 4 2-6-0 climbs towards Windsor Hill Tunnel

FROM THE FOOTPLATE

GA

At Windsor Hill tunnel we must be very careful with a passenger train which is travelling down the bank at close to 60mph. For a split second as the engine enters the tunnel at that speed it creates a partial vacuum where the engine has literally filled the tunnel and the air has nowhere to go, apart from being pushed forward in front of the engine.

The air is then forced back under the engine up into the ash pan and into the fire. If the fire box door is left open and the blower full on (The blower manages the draft of air flowing from the back of the boiler through the tubes and out the chimney and helps complete combustion of the fuel by supplying oxygen) then flames shoot out from the firebox at least 2 foot long into the cab. Entering the tunnel, we stand well clear of the firebox, and we only suffer popping ears once or twice.

On reaching Shepton Mallet the track crosses two viaducts. The first is the 118-yard-long Bath Road Viaduct and carries the line across the B3136 road. The viaduct stands 62ft high and is the highest on the Somerset & Dorset Railway.

In a short time, we cross the impressive 27 arched Charlton Viaduct sweeping in a gentle curve for 317 yards, the longest on the Somerset & Dorset Railway, before running into the busy station.

SHEPTON MALLET 9.32am

FROM BATH GREEN PARK 21¾ Miles

DISTANCE TO BOURNEMOUTH 49¾ Miles

The station was renamed Shepton Mallet (Charlton Road) in October 1883 to avoid confusion with the GWR station. The main station buildings are located on the up platform and contain the Station Masters Office, Booking Office, a Booking Hall and both a Ladies and Gentleman's Waiting Room.

On the down platform is a small waiting room and the signal box. Access to both platforms is provided by a girder footbridge. At the end of the down platform is the water crane. The sidings at Shepton Mallet are extensive and create a busy scene with a stone crushing plant, a goods shed, cattle dock, general traffic sidings and a 5-ton yard crane.

Immediately after leaving the station the train passes under the GWR branch line from Witham to Wells. There is a brief climb out from Shepton Mallet before the descent from the Mendips continues unabated at 1.50 for the next 7 miles or so. Shepton Mallet is an important station and freight locomotive on the up road take on water here before commencing the steep climb over the Mendip Hills to Binegar

S&D Class 7F No 53807 taking on water at Shepton Mallet

FROM THE FOOTPLATE

WM

The staff at Shepton mallet are very helpful including boiling the kettle for us to top up the tea can.

I can recall the first time I travelled to Shepton Mallet on S&D class 7F freight locomotive No.13800, later re-numbered 53800, and looking between the sleepers to the road 60 feet below. I shouted to the driver that the arch support had disappeared and moved to the driver's side of the footplate to find all the platelayers pressing themselves against the up-line parapet wall. My driver who was Aubrey was busy talking to the pilot man, Binegar Station master Norman Down, who was there because only one line, the up line, was in use due to the down line having collapsed.

The up-line viaduct had previously fallen and been replaced. It was some months later that I worked out in my mind that each line was supported on separate viaducts as the original line had been doubled.

With doubling of the track, the Bath Road viaduct was widened on the western side and built of brick. The area between the two separate structures was causing concern due to leaking water. In February 1946 the middle section of the new viaduct gave way, but fortunately there was no train crossing and no loss of life. Trains were running again the next day with a temporary skewed track and a speed restriction imposed. Normal service resumed in August, but further remedial work had to be carried out on the viaduct a year later with temporary single line working reintroduced.

PRESTLEIGH VIADUCT

S&D Class 7F No 53808 passes north over Prestleigh Viaduct

Between Shepton Mallet and Evercreech the line curves gently over open countryside and passes over the graceful stone structure of the eleven arch viaduct close to the village of Prestleigh.

FROM THE FOOTPLATE

WM

We had taken over an engine at Norton Hill Colliery during the coal shortage. The engine had already completed one journey from Bath to Evercreech Junction but there were no lumps left to build up the fire for the next journey back to Evercreech Junction. The tender was half full of water sloshing about the small amount of coal and cement that remained. I tried to create a hole to enable water to escape but without success until that was, we came to a halt at Prestleigh Viaduct. Due to a brake hanger and broken brake block becoming jammed over the wheel under the outer footplate. We had to hammer it free before we could continue. Whilst on the viaduct the loose water on the tender broke free washing every speck of briquette dust overboard as we headed to Evercreech Junction. We then had to look around for coal to use for the return journey.

EVERCREECH NEW 9.40am

FROM BATH GREEN PARK 24¾ Miles

DISTANCE TO BOURNEMOUTH 46¾ Miles

The station here at Evercreech New was opened on 20 July 1874 when the Bath Extension was completed. The new station is now well situated for the large Somerset village, far more convenient than the original one at Evercreech Junction some 2 miles away to the south. Sited on the western end of the village it was initially called Evercreech Village.

The down platform houses the main station buildings built in the traditional style although the shelter on the up platform is more substantial than most, being built of stone. The signal box next to the shelter is a rebuilt version dating from 1920, the original destroyed by fire in 1918. The main building houses the Station Masters Office Booking Office and separate Ladies and Gentleman's Waiting Rooms. Just two sidings, one on the up line serving a limestone works and a local milk factory, with the down siding housing the goods shed and a travelling crane.

The view from the signal box as BR Class 4 2-6-0 No 76019 approaches the up platform

Ex- GWR Collett 0-6-0 No. 3218 passing the North Box at Evercreech Junction with a milk train from Bason Bridge to Templecombe. The branch line to Burnham-on-Sea, which was once the original Somerset Central Railway, can be seen running straight into the distance. The extension to Bath, now the main line, turns away in a sharp curve north-eastward

EVERCREECH JUNCTION 9.46am

FROM BATH GREEN PARK 26½ Miles

DISTANCE TO BOURNEMOUTH 45 Miles

Approaching Evercreech Junction, the descent from the Mendips continues as the train slows to negotiate the tight left-hand curve as the line converges alongside the straight line to Burnham- on-Sea, reflecting that it was the original line.

The attractive main building is located on the down platform along with the Station Masters House. The two platforms are connected by means of a footbridge located between the house and the northern signal box, one of two at the junction. The unusually tall signal box built of timber and brick allows a view over the footbridge and is located next to the level crossing, controlling the A371 Shepton Mallet to Castle Cary Road.

The station was originally named just Evercreech in 1862 when it first opened but soon became known as Evercreech Junction with the new opening of the Bath Extension, with the village of Evercreech acquiring the second station. This station served as the Burnham-on-Sea branch of the Burnham to Broadstone line for the original Somerset & Dorset Joint Railway. At that time, it was the main line before the northward's extension, a decision that eventually bankrupted company.

The junction has always been a very busy place evidenced by the many sidings and two large signal boxes and turntable. To the north of the station is the large six road marshalling yard and the numerous other sidings including private sidings for the Somerset Tile & Brick Company. Shunting in the busy yards which house a 7-ton crane can continue day and night. The 56ft turntable installed in 1934 replaced an earlier smaller table as was the case at Bath. The turntable is located between the two separating main lines to Burnham-on-Sea and Evercreech New. The turntable is large enough to turn the S&D Class 7F although it is unable to accommodate the BR Class 9F.

All trains of eight or more coaches must be assisted on the climb over the Mendip Hills from Evercreech Junction, all that is except for the class 9F. Many locomotives can be seen lined up on the middle road particularly on Saturday mornings during the busy summer season.

A wet day at Evercreech Junction as BR Class 4 2-6-0 No 76015 sets off from Evercreech Junction on the short climb to Evercreech New ahead of the gruelling climb back over the Mendip Hills

FROM THE FOOTPLATE

GA

At Evercreech Junction we stop to take on water. It is here that the pilot engine used on the double headers from Bath drops off after assisting us over the Mendip Hills, and we continue on our own to Bournemouth. While we take on water at Evercreech Junction I get up on the tender and catch hold of large lumps of coal and place them all along the edge of the side of the tender. After taking on water, we cross over the level crossing and head down the long straight. Now just after a mile or so we run over two little country level crossings next to two small cottages.

The people who live in the cottages open the gates for us to go through. Now the little cottages have coal fires, but they are only limited to a certain amount of coal that British Rail allows them, hence the lumps on the side of the tender. I get back upon the tender, currently we are doing about 40mph, and kick off the coal so it lands in the path of a chap waiting there with a wheelbarrow. Every now and again we get a basket of fruit and veg from him on the way back. From here on it's all plain sailing to Templecombe.

FROM THE FOOTPLATE

WM

My home loco shed is at Radstock with foreman Charles Baker supported by Harold Morris, shed master at Bath locomotive depot, an outstanding able boss. During summer timetable working the Radstock staff must go to Bath to work the excursion and summer specials. The Bath tunnels (Devonshire and Combe Down) have smoke and steam emitting from both ends from Friday midnight through to 4/5pm on a Saturday. I hate these tunnels and if I had to work on that section regularly, I would leave the service.

On one occasion I was teamed up with a Bath driver at the last minute on the 9am Sunshine Express to Bournemouth with a holiday excursion from Bath with an Armstrong Whitworth 0-6-0 locomotive. Without small pony wheels these engines were rough travellers and unsuitable for fast speeds.

On the return journey passing over the Cole curve, at restricted speed, the driver put all his weight on the brass injector steam valve control wheel to steady himself, but the valve spindle gave way, the wheel came off, and the driver was thrown across the footplate in front of me. I threw myself towards him and managed to trap one of his feet against the tender handrail.

The two of us struggled to get him back on board just in time for him to stop at Evercreech Junction. He never said thanks. Amen. And I expect never again drove that route for a long time.

BR Class 4 2-6-0 No 76027 running into the junction about to pass over the level crossing. The tall signal box controls the gates on the A371. The line recedes into the distance following a gentler course towards Templecombe

COLE FOR BRUTON 9.54am

FROM BATH GREEN PARK 29¼ Miles
DISTANCE TO BOURNEMOUTH 42¼ Miles

Cole for Bruton was originally the northern most station on the Dorset Central Railway which amalgamated with the Somerset Central Railway to form the Somerset & Dorset Railway in 1862.

The main station building, located on the down platform, is built in the archetypal Dorset style with high gable ends and tall chimneys and no canopy. The small signal box, built in the recognisable style of the L & S.W.R. and a small wooden shelter are housed on the up platform.

The station is signed Cole for Bruton due the proximity of the town. As the train leaves the rural station it continues over unspoilt countryside with a brief return to climbing for the next 4 miles or so to reach the town of Wincanton.

WINCANTON 10.03am

FROM BATH GREEN PARK 33½ Miles

DISTANCE TO BOURNEMOUTH 38 Miles

Wincanton station opened in November 1861, by the Dorset Central Railway, has two staggered platforms, the up platform being over twice the length of the down.

The nearby racecourse creates a lot of horse traffic and passenger traffic on race days. The traditional main station buildings with a canopy are located on the smaller down platform with a small wooden shelter and signal box on the longer up platform.

The goods area is situated to the south of the station where Cow & Gate have their own siding for tankers to be taken by rail to London via Templecombe. Access between platforms is provided by means of a concrete footbridge.

TEMPLECOMBE 10.13am

FROM BATH GREEN PARK 37 Miles
DISTANCE TO BOURNEMOUTH 34½ Miles

Passing Templecombe Junction 2 we are now close to the end of the double track joining what was the original single track Dorset Central line for the next 16 miles to Blanford Forum. From there the line doubles again to Broadstone ahead of reaching Bournemouth.

Once onto the single line working there is a very small platform with no station buildings set between two bridges, the southern bridge carrying the Exeter to Waterloo line. However, the platform is no longer used as stopping trains continue onto the spur back at Junction 2 calling at Templecombe Upper Station on the Waterloo to Exeter route.

The train halts at the island platform allowing passengers to change for other destinations. A subway provides safe access from the island platform to a substantial main station situated on the southern side of the junction.

Continuing to Bournemouth on the Somerset & Dorset is a somewhat laborious affair as once ready to continue an engine is attached at the rear of the complete train. The complete train, locomotive as well, is hauled backwards to junction 2. The pulling engine uncouples allowing the train to continue the journey to Bournemouth joining the single track and continuing under the London Waterloo to Exeter main line just past the single platform.

Up trains from Bournemouth to Bath must stop just beyond junction 2 and another engine is coupled to the rear. This time the whole train is hauled back into the station. The pulling engine uncouples allowing the train, when ready, to move off freely to rejoin the Somerset & Dorset Railway back at Junction 2.

Through trains to Bournemouth including the Pines Express and those not scheduled to call at Templecombe continue straight onto the single line.

Extensive sidings and a Locomotive Power Depot are located here at Templecombe.

FROM THE FOOTPLATE

GA

With an excursion train of up to twelve coaches we don't stop at Templecombe, we continue onto the single line by taking the tablet at Templecombe Lower signal box and run down beside Templecombe shed. We then continue onto Blandford passing through Henstridge, Stalbridge, Sturminster Newton and Shillingstone, before arriving at Blanford.

Depending where the loop is on the stations between Templecombe and Blanford we can pick up the tablet for the next single line sections at up to 60mph. We must make sure to give a tablet and catch a new tablet which permits the engine to enter the next single line section.

If you blink you can miss it and the tablet could be sent spinning up into the air, which has never happened to me. We would then have to put on full brake application, and on a twelve-coach train it will take 1½ miles to stop. It is then down to the fireman to walk the 1½ miles back to the station to find it, because if you've lost it all the tablet apparatus in the signal box is automatically locked. An electrician would then have to be called out from Bristol, so if you missed the tablet, it would create havoc.

On our stopping train we are now hauled back to Somerset & Dorset rails and continue south for another 34½ miles, travelling through some magnificent pastoral Dorset countryside.

S&D Class 7F No 53804 sets off on the single line section from No 2 Junction. The spur can be seen on the left gaining height to reach the level of the London Waterloo to Exeter line station at Templecombe

HENSTRIDGE 10.20am

FROM BATH GREEN PARK 38¾ Miles

DISTANCE TO BOURNEMOUTH 32¾ Miles

Our next stop is in the tiny village of Henstridge. The station here is the smallest on the main line with just a single platform on the upside and no passing loop. The Booking Office and Ladies and Gentleman's Waiting Rooms are contained in a wooden building with no canopy. When the Pines Express roars through the station the buildings literally vibrate.

There is a level crossing serving a minor road and a single siding for goods controlled by a ground frame as there is no signal box at Henstridge.

In ¾ of a mile heading south the train crosses over the border from Somerset into Dorset.

STALBRIDGE 10.25am

FROM BATH GREEN PARK 40¼ Miles
DISTANCE TO BOURNEMOUTH 31¼ Miles

The station buildings at Stalbridge are brick built, in stark contrast to the mellow limestone on the many attractive stations over the Mendips. Built in the traditional Dorset style with high gables and tall chimneys they are situated on the up platform where there is the Station Masters House, the main station building with the Booking Office and the Waiting Rooms, but no canopy. The signal box is located next to a minor road and controls the level crossing.

Evening Star heading north calls at Sturminster Newton

STURMINSTER NEWTON 10.33am

FROM BATH GREEN PARK 44¼ Miles

DISTANCE TO BOURNEMOUTH 27¾ Miles

Continuing south through the beautiful Stour Valley we cross a lattice girder bridge crossing the River Stour reaching the station at Sturminster Newton through a deep rock cutting.

As at Stalbridge the station buildings follow in the style of the Dorset Central Railway but with staggered platforms. The standard offices are located on the up platform which is unusual as there is a dip in the middle. The dip enables passengers to cross the line on a wooden crossing as there is no footbridge, like many of the station on the Somerset & Dorset Railway

The busy market town is served with extensive sidings complete with a brick-built goods shed. A traditional loop allows trains to pass on this single line section with the up road having the straight run. The signal box here is a simple wooden affair.

SHILLINGSTONE 10.40am

FROM BATH GREEN PARK 47¼ Miles
DISTANCE TO BOURNEMOUTH 24¼ Miles

Passing over the River Stour once more we run into Shillngstone. The buildings are again in the style of the Dorset Central Railway but with the addition of an ornate canopy, rather unusual for the southern region. It is believed to have been built for the visit of King Edward VII. The main buildings are located on the up platform within the passing loop. A basic wooden shelter on the down platform provides passenger protection from the elements. There is a small timber built signal box on the up platform within the passing loop.

The gardens are particularly well tended and have won many 'Best Kept' awards over the years.

BLANFORD FORUM 10.54am

FROM BATH GREEN PARK 52¾ Miles
DISTANCE TO BOURNEMOUTH 18¾ Miles

The station at Blandford Forum is the largest on the line with the single line running from Templecombe reverting to double track for the next 8 miles to Corfe Mullen. Situated central to the town the station follows the style of the Dorset Central Railway but on a much grander scale.

The large brick buildings on the up platform provide shelter with a generous canopy. Included is a large Booking Office. A subway provides access to both platforms on this busy section of Southern Region track. The goods yard is located on the downside with a generous goods sheds and cattle pens. An unusually tall signal box along with a very substantial shelter are located on the up platform.

BAILEY GATE 11.12am

FROM BATH GREEN PARK 60 Miles
DISTANCE TO BOURNEMOUTH 11½ Miles

Bailey Gate is for the most part a freight depot more so than a passenger station. When it was opened in 1860 it was initially known as Sturminster Marshall but to save confusion the name was changed to Bailey Gate, named after a local farm. The extensive sidings serve the milk and cheese industries with regular freight trains running to London via Templecombe. The United Dairies factory has grown to be one of the greatest producers of Cheddar cheese in the world. It has also become one of the largest in the UK for transporting milk by rail, carried in tanker wagons to London. Watercress is also delivered on the Somerset & Dorset via Bath to the north of England.

The station buildings include a Waiting Room and Ticket Office on the downside.

On the up platform is a small wooden hut used as a Waiting Room with a wooden signal box adjacent to the sidings. Access to the station is by means of a wooden sleeper style crossing. Shortly after leaving the station the line has to cross the busy A371 Wimborne to Dorchester Road at Bailey Gate Crossing, controlled by the brick and timber built signal box on the downside of the line.

FROM THE FOOTPLATE

GA

The excursion makes a stop at Blanford before continuing the run down into Poole. Travelling to Poole there is a long straight near Bailey Gate with a track coming off from the Wimborne line. This section had been renewed with concrete sleepers and flat-bottomed rails so on one occasion we were determined to see if we could get 75mph out of our standard engine. We roared down this long straight watching the speed going up and could see the curve at the bottom of the straight leading onto the Wimborne line getting closer and closer.

Knowing that if we had been doing anywhere near 75mph when we reached the points we would derail so we left it as long as we could and slammed on the brake, hoping we would take the points at under 30mph, which thankfully we did.

BROADSTONE   11.25am

FROM BATH GREEN PARK 63½ Miles

DISTANCE TO BOURNEMOUTH 8 Miles

Single line working returns for 3 miles between Corfe Mullen and Broadstone and includes a 1½ mile climb of 1.80 passing a sand cutting bordered by pine trees.

Broadstone marks the end of single line working, originally named New Poole Junction when opened in June 1847. The large station is however really the end of the line as far as the Somerset & Dorset is concerned, the remainder of the 8 miles or so to Bournemouth will be over old L.S.W.R. Southern Region track.

Three generous platforms seem to dominate the station buildings with access by means of a substantial covered footbridge. The Station Masters Office is located on the island platform with the Booking Office on the main down platform.

The station buildings are timber clad but have significant tall ornate chimneys, somewhat out of keeping.

Leaving Broadstone the line descends at 1.75 and in 2 miles we reach Holes Bay, with the sea now in sight. The line is soon joined from the left by the Weymouth to Waterloo line. At Poole all trains must stop.

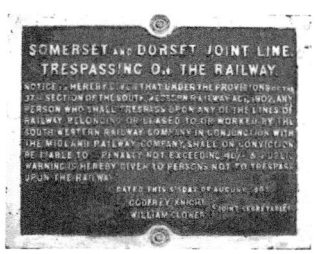

FROM THE FOOTPLATE

GA

At Poole the station is on a left-hand curve and around the corner is a level crossing in the town centre and a metal bridge for pedestrians for when the gates are closed.

We then run up Parkstone Bank on double track through a deep cutting, on our own un-assisted, with twelve coaches on. When we had a green back, which is a Southern Railways West Country class locomotive, the civil engineer from Southampton got on the phone to Bath Green Park saying that we have no rights to leave Poole without an assisting engine.

He claimed there is no way we could get up the bank to Branksome with just one engine pulling twelve coaches. We took no notice because we go up the bank on our own regardless of which engine we have.

BOURNEMOUTH WEST 11.53am

FROM BATH GREEN PARK 71½ Miles

After leaving Poole Station and passing over two level crossings the gradient briefly increases to 1.60 to Branksome before falling at 1.90 on the final run into Bournemouth West, some 71½ miles from Bath Green Park.

We arrive safely at Bournemouth West at 11.53am, just in time for lunch on the sea front, that is if I can find my sandwiches and flask.

Bournemouth West was opened in 1874. As well as the terminus for the Somerset & Dorset the station is used by trains coming in from London Waterloo and other local services from Weymouth and Swanage, handy to explore the Dorset coast. The station is located inside the Hampshire border by ½ a mile.

FROM THE FOOTPLATE

GA

Approaching Bournemouth, the line continues towards Christchurch and Bournemouth Central while we branch right to go to Bournemouth West. At this point the track forms a triangle allowing trains coming from Bournemouth Central to run directly into Bournemouth West.

When we run down into Bournemouth the coaches are taken off us as it is a dead end like Bath Green Park. We then run the engine back, tender first, 1½ miles up the long straight, and run around the triangle to turn the engine so that it is facing the right way to return to Bath. Inside the triangle is Branksome locomotive shed where we coal the engine and drop the fire. This is where the Branksome men sign on for work.

When we get to the shed, I pull the coal forward take on water and add coal to the fire. We then go down and have a wash and change our clothes. We have a small suitcase with us when we are on what is called a short rest, in other words on a twelve-hour shift.

WM

On one occasion arriving at Bournemouth West on a Saturday our guard, Mr Ted Frances, who later became Inspector Frances at Bath informed us of two immediate problems. First the triangle used for turning locomotives for the return journey could not be accessed as materials for major track improvements on Sunday were stored on the track. Secondly the turntable at Bournemouth Central was difficult to use and there was a string of engines' waiting to turn.

So the problem remained. The driver asked me if I was prepared to travel back to Evercreech Junction, tender first, where we could then turn the engine. Finding a tarpaulin to give limited shelter and having a good steaming engine I agreed, knowing this was unusual and uncomfortable for passengers affected by coal dust.

At Evercreech Junction we turned the engine and continued to Bath Green Park in the customary way.

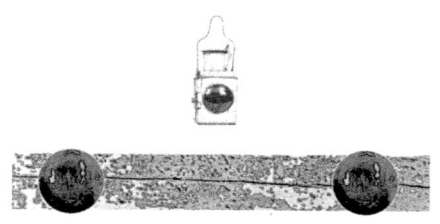

PART TWO

JUST LIKE MY DREAMS

PREFACE

Imagine if you could, no Beeching, Marples or Bahramov, well why not take a journey on the 17.42 evening commuter DMU service form Bath Green Park to Evercreech Junction, calling at all stations, circa mid-1980s. Then a swift change to continue our journey west to Burnham-On-Sea'

In 1966 British Railways withdrew steam hauled services from the Somerset & Dorset and replaced them with diesel locomotion opening a new world, journey times were reduced and with more frequent trains it was now possible to visit London for the day.

Sit back and enjoy the journey as we glide effortlessly over the Mendips in a short story from 2019.

BATH GREEN PARK

The station announcers articulate voice resonates into the serene warm early evening air..........*"The train now departing platform one is the 17.42 to Evercreech Junction, stopping at all stations"*.

Scarcely made it on time but here I am on the packed early evening commuter service form Bath Green Park. Nevertheless, much better than having to battle my way home through the traffic congestion on the A367, notoriously dire at Radstock in the early evening. Still, I should be home in under half an hour. Just as a side note, if I had missed this train there is always the 18.05 special I could take.

The still atmosphere at Bath Green Park belies its position in the centre of the bustling Georgian City with the two platforms in constant use throughout the day, now serving the line southward to Evercreech Junction with the opportunity to continue southwards to Bournemouth or west to Burnham-on-Sea.

Bristol Temple Meads is now a short travel time away with a connection nowadays with the mainline from London put in place about two miles west out from Bath Green Park.

The original link on the old Midland line running in from Bristol now provides the choice of two routes into Bristol.

The station building has been wonderfully restored with the stonework back to its pristine condition, any trace of the build-up of almost a century of smoke completely removed.

I have no time this evening to draw on the superb facilities the station now offers, but today the railway passenger can take advantage of an extensive restaurant, tea/coffee shop and the traditional railway station newsagents, selling far more than newspapers. There is also a generous size comfortable waiting room and a flower seller always on hand should an occasion arise.

The elegant facade retains a large booking office, post office and a tourist information centre.

Blue is the colour at the present time, quite a change of character from the blood and custard days of steam. The vaulted glass roof is gleaming allowing the early evening summer sun to stream through, adding to the rather serene atmosphere for a busy railway terminal. That said one always compares the present to the halcyon days of steam, dominated by the noise of the living engines and the air heavy from the combustion fumes.

The announcer today would have had some boisterous competition back in the 60s.

The skyline of the city has changed very little since the days of steam. Although the infrastructure has been modernised low level building has managed to preserve the beautiful Georgian city. Conversely major development has taken place to the west of the station buildings, once the home of the four-road engine shed.

The substantial wooden building has been replaced with the modern-day equivalent built of clinical steel, now housing a vast distribution centre.

The turntable has long gone, a bye product of steam as the modern engines no longer require turning, saving a significant amount of time for trains running in from the north.

A significant area of the extensive goods yard has been handed over to serve the very productive Somerset Coalfields. New road and rail networks have been put in place to enable the thirty-foot container wagons laden with coal to be transferred direct to lorries for road haulage.

Shunting continues into the night, readying the consignments for their onward journey from the regular goods trains arriving overloaded with hopper wagons from the coalfields. Just one diesel engine will haul these massive payloads to the major industrial coal depots throughout the country.

There are several private sidings now catering for the growing retail outlets in the city as well as conveying raw materials. The sidings also act as distributions channels for the long-established and new manufacturers that have sprung up outside the city, due in the main to the far-reaching rail connections.

We glide with ease, and almost without sound, from under the single span vaulted glass roof before taking the track left, leaving behind the vast goods yard at Bath Junction.

Bath Junction is a token exchange point where the train enters single track working through to Midford, the driver reports the trains position to a signaller by radio and requests the token for the next section of line ahead. If the signaller can do so an electronic token is issued. At the same time the driver must press a button in the cab to receive the token. The token is then transmitted to the train by radio.

The system prevents the issue of a token that would allow more than one train in a single line section at any one time. This system replaced the manual token exchange so prominent in the days of steam.

The system originated from a remote line in the far north of Scotland. The line was controlled by traditional electric exchange token instruments, but severe weather disrupted over 40 miles of track.

The radio link was the simplest, quickest and the most cost-efficient way to restore the service. A feasibility study of using radio to affect the token combined with the use of voice communication between signaller and driver effectively removed the need for staffed signal boxes, by moving the instruments into the cab of the train.

The gradient now increases and so does our speed as we begin the climb to the two tunnels.

The first, Devonshire Tunnel, is soon upon us as the light fades to darkness for a short time, soon returning to the warm glow of the early evening sun lighting up Lyncombe vale. In a wink of an eye the darkness returns as we pass through the mile or so of Combe Down Tunnel.

In the darkness I can see my reflection in the glass as the tunnel wall speeds past, and I ponder stories told by the old Somerset & Dorset drivers and fireman of how they had to cope with the climb out of Bath.

No comfortable cab to sit in for them as the driver has today, coasting through the tunnels almost unnoticed.

They often told tales of how they had to get down on their hands and knees with a cloth over their face and gasp for breath with the footplate on the slow-moving engine awash with intense heat, smoke and sulphur fumes.

As we emerge from the tunnel the warm glow of the summer sun returns and we are met with delightful fleeting glimpses of the beautiful Somerset countryside, and there lies one of the drawbacks of diesel over steam, the speed that the views pass by.

MIDFORD HALT

Seated on the left of the carriage the impressive viaduct comes into view as we ease into the station. Sadly, the delightful wooden building, including the signal box, have been demolished and replaced with a modern shelter standing isolated on the upside.

The iconic signal box became surplus to requirement with the introduction of the radio-controlled token exchange system that allowed us to travel the single line section from Bath Junction to Midford.

Immediately after the station the track reverts to double line working over the viaduct. The GWR that ran under the viaduct is now a distant reminder, the track bed overgrown by vegetation. The once busy goods yard, like the signal box, is now a distant memory. Midford was downgraded to a halt but is fundamental for commuters with its short travel time from the centre of Bath.

A review carried out by the government of the day in 1963 titled The Reshaping of British Railways recommended that some stations on rural lines be downgraded to a halt.

The proposals led to a substantial reduction in staffing levels. However, fear was rife at one point that the report could recommend the closure of rural lines due to lack of passenger numbers.

These uncertainties were soon allayed when surveys carried out during morning and evening times demonstrated the need for these services to remain in place, therefore reducing the burden on the already increasing traffic on country roads.

I can never pass through Midford and not be reminded of the delightful 1950s British comedy, 'The Titfield Thunderbolt'.

Midford Halt is a popular stopping off point for walkers, the station on the Somerset Wiltshire border is just over two miles west from Limpley Stoke, and the Kennet & Avon Canal with its renowned Dundas Aqueduct.

WELLOW

It was but a fleeting stop at Midford and we are off again, coasting with ease from the unembellished station we cross the B3110 on the eight-arch viaduct towards Wellow.

We leave behind the single line working and its double track all the way to our destination at Evercreech Junction. For the next two miles we follow close to the Wellow Brook through the delightful pastoral Somerset countryside.

Running into the station here at Wellow it seems almost unreal that less than ten minutes ago we were in the centre of Bath. In stark contrast to Midford the traditional Somerset & Dorset limestone building have remained intact, and it would be difficult to tell if it was still 1966, a time lest hasty than our own, or the present-day.

The only victim of modern-day running is the goods yard and sidings that nowadays see little use. The restricted road links to the village and surrounding area have hampered progressive transportation, with local freight now centred at Radstock.

Wellow has managed to retain its status as a station rather than a halt although the staffing levels have been greatly reduced since the passing of steam.

The well frequented commuter station has retained its glorious Somerset & Dorset aura with no small thanks to a band of retired volunteers who manage the gardens and ensure the building are kept looking pristine.

SHOSCOMBE HALT

The halt of Shoscombe & Single Hill was shortened to just Shoscombe Halt shortly after the changes came into place in 1966. No reason was given although it has been suggested it was just necessary to be able incorporate the station name with ease into the new timetable.

The halt is one of the least used on the line, but it came as a relief for the small number of passengers when it was announced it would remain open. The narrow country lanes restrict any potential bus services in the area.

Our evening commuter train pauses briefly at the halt and barely a couple of passengers alight before coasting towards Radstock where considerable changes post steam ere have taken place.

RADSTOCK JUNCTION

The new infrastructure at Radstock has amalgamated the old Somerset & Dorset and GWR railway lines into one station. The centre of Radstock has undergone major work with the busy A367 re-routed through an underpass to avoid the tail backs so evident in the days of steam.

Now re-named Radstock Junction it is possible to interchange and take the train to Westbury for London or south to Salisbury and Southampton via Frome. Travel north-west and the lines meanders to Bristol.

1966 will always be a year to remember, not least for the relief felt by many when British Rail released their findings of its report into the future of railways with the recommendation to retain the majority of its rural services.

It was also an epic year in the field of sport with England hosting the World Cup Finals for the first time. On the 29th of July on a hot summers day the final was contested between the hosts and West Germany at Wembley Stadium.

Fortunately, I was able to travel by rail to Bath Green Park. No direct connection at that time to London from Radstock as we enjoy today, so a short hop across Bath and I board the train from Bath Spa.

Once at Wembley Stadium I take up a position behind the goal, the ticket cost me ten shillings, not bad at today's prices. I am surrounded by both England and West German supporters all determined to have a great day out whatever the result.

The game in now in full flow and soon the unthinkable happens, West Germany score. Still plenty of time left. GOAL........... England equalise after 18 minutes courtesy of a free kick by Bobby Moore straight onto the head of his West Ham teammate Geoff Hurst.

The second half is now well underway, and this is turning out to be a good game of football. Activity in the West German penalty area leads to a second goal for England, this time from another West Ham man, Martin Peters.

Just seconds to go now and West Germany are awarded a free kick just outside the England penalty area. The worst happens and West Germany equalise, now it's 2-2 and we will get an extra unwanted 30 minutes to do it all again.

Eleven minutes into extra time Hurst fires a shot from within the penalty area goal-wards. The shot bounced sharply off the underside of the bar and hit the ground before spinning backwards away from the goal. Was it in? The England players seemed to think so, but then Swiss referee Deinst seemed unsure.

The referee went across to consult with the replacement linesman, who stood in at the last minute for Tofig Bahramov. There followed a long period of indecision before eventually deciding that the ball had not crossed the line.

The match finally ended 2-2 with no people coming onto the pitch and a replay the following Wednesday evening arranged back at Wembley. I had to be content to watch the match on television.

Prior to the stations combining Radstock North on the old S&D line had run parallel to the GWR but was never connected.

The bold decision to integrate to form one main station has created a modern terminus with both lines served by the addition of an island platform. A subway for passenger transfers has replaced the original footbridge.

The name change to Radstock Junction imparts how significant a development this has become.

Passenger numbers have grown far more than what planners had envisaged with commuters now able to travel to Bristol, Bath, Frome and even London daily.

The goods yard is a hive of activity around the clock with coal being the most transported commodity. The wagon works has grown now serving a large part of British Rail Southern Region stock, thanks in the main to the easy rail access afforded with the amalgamation.

The A367 underpass has removed the need for level crossing gates, and the pedestrian area is controlled by automatic barriers. So much has changed here at Radstock since 1966.

The original signal box has been dismantled and replaced with a modern structure located at the eastern end of the long island platform, adjacent to the busy good yard.

It's a mere seventeen minutes since we left the centre of Bath on the early evening commuter service calling at all stations, running through to Evercreech Junction.

We continue the course of the old Somerset & Dorset climbing to reach the North Somerset Viaduct. Here we cross over the A362 and the line meandering via the small platform at Midsomer Norton Halt to Pensford with its impressive sixteen arch viaduct, ahead of reaching Bristol.

Little has changed track side since the days of steam as we climb towards Midsomer Norton South Station aside from the bushes and trees that have now smothered the line side banks.

MIDSOMER NORTON SOUTH

We soon reach the industrious sidings of Norton Hill Colliery that have continued to thrive with the greatly improved rail access developed since the late 1960s. We then cross the B3355 before running into the station over the new automatic level crossing.

The station buildings, including the signal box and iconic Somerset & Dorset wooden shelter, all remain intact and in pristine condition, no small thanks to a band of volunteers here at Midsomer Norton South.

The station is home to The Somerset & Dorset Steam Heritage Trust, set up by a team of volunteers to preserve the halcyon days of steam on the Somerset & Dorset Railway. The last steam service withdrawn in March 1966 was replaced by diesel traction.

The trust has converted the old stable block into a museum dedicated to the Somerset & Dorset prior to 7th March 1966.

Through various fundraising activities and generous donations, the trust managed to salvage and restore a BR Class 4MT 2-6-4 locomotive. The locomotive is now housed in the old engine shed. Three Mk1 maroon carriages, owned by the trust stand on the once busy sidings which are no longer used by British Rail. All freight activity is now centred at Radstock Junction.

With unique permission from British Rail the trust is able to operate a steam service between here and Binegar at least half a dozen times throughout the year, an event that draws thousands of visitors to the area, with tickets always sold well in advance.

As well as use by commuters Midsomer Norton South continues to serve as a vital focal point for the Mendip villages with large numbers of school children arriving and departing during term time at the secondary schools in the town.

Post steam era the B3355 was realigned to allow an automatic half-barrier crossing to be installed consisting of a single arm each side of the road which blocks only oncoming traffic, leaving the exits clear.

The controlled level crossing replaced the very low bridge that severely affected traffic into and out of Midsomer Norton from the south.

The major work to overcome the height restriction was more than welcome by the carnival association now that Midsomer Norton is part of the Somerset carnival circuit.

Once a year extra trains transport scores of passengers into the town, from Bath in the north and Bournemouth in the south, to celebrate one of the most exciting displays of illuminated entertainment.

In addition, the railway allows easy access to the other carnivals on the circuit at Wells, Glastonbury and Burnham-on-Sea from Evercreech Junction.

In the days of steam fully loaded trains would toil to pull away from the station as the gradient increases immediately to 1 in 55 at the end of the platform where the track curves towards Chilcompton.

The relentless gradient is now with us until we reach Masbury summit, but our engine moves off with ease from the station continuing south to Chilcompton, passing without ceremony through the twin bored Chilcompton Tunnel.

The tunnel was always a popular spot for photographers during the age of steam. Double headers had to battle the extreme gradient through the tunnel on the down line, emerging in a halo of steam above the Mendip village.

CHILCOMPTON

As our train glides effortlessly past Chilcompton rock cutting the former S&D station comes into sight. Much has changed since the days of the 'Double Header' steam trains chugging their way up the relentless 1 in 55 gradients, ahead of the short respite of 1 in 300 through the station.

Without doubt the most notable absentee are the large stone-built water towers that dominated the south aspect of the station.

The familiar Mendip line-side wooden clad water towers have long gone, nevertheless the infrastructure has developed to include additional sidings to facilitate coal from the thriving New Rock colliery.

The Somerset coalfield is now one of the most productive in the country. The busy sawmill that dominates the village now has its own siding running parallel to the south of the station, where the water towers once stood.

Once a day a heavily laden goods train consisting of up to ten four wheeled thirty-foot container wagons and several hopper wagons departs Chilcompton. The payload is coal destined for onward distribution from the goods yard at Bath Green Park. The containers are lifted onto lorries with the hopper wagons routed to a major industrial coal depot.

The main station building has survived, with the shelter on the up platform reminiscent of a bus stop, having replaced the traditional wooden structure. The original signal box is used to marshal the busy goods yard.

Timber from the sawmill and concrete products from the local stone company are distributed by goods train up to three times a week. Watercress is dispatched to Bath for distribution throughout Britain and beyond, freshness is ensured with the commodity carried on the scheduled passenger services to Bath.

The station provides an essential commuter service for Chilcompton and the surrounding villages to Bath, as can be witnessed by the number of cars parked at the station during the week. Increasing numbers now take the 07.46 early morning commuter service running from Evercreech Junction to Bath Green Park.

The reduced journey time now takes twenty-five minutes from Chilcompton compared to forty-five during the leisurely days of steam. During term time the 08.10 to Bath provides a vital link for pupils attending the two Secondary schools in Midsomer Norton.

From mid-afternoon to early evening the station is a busy place, at first with returning school children and commuters from Bath, Radstock and Midsomer Norton arriving home.

The gardens are sadly a vague reminder of the halcyon days of steam due in no small part to the staffing levels greatly reduced, with just a ticket officer and the signalman on part time duty.

It's now 18.07, just 25 minutes out from Bath and running on time, the train glides with ease from the station continuing to climb over the Mendip Hills.

The next station on the journey is Binegar ahead of reaching the summit at Masbury. Trains no longer stop at Masbury since the passing of steam, fortunately the only station on the old Bath extension to be closed.

We pass by Moorewood sidings located between Chilcompton and Binegar which continue to serve the Mendip Stone Works at Emborough. A heavily laden weekly freight train can be seen hauling loaded wagons, with ease form the sidings for an onward journey to London.

Imagine if all the freight sent by rail had to be carried over the already busy country roads, you could get held up for an age taking a simple journey into Bath.

BINEGAR

What was always seen as a relentless couple of miles or so during the age of steam has now become an effortless glide, how the fireman who had to keep the engine stoked would relish sitting in the warm cab today.

Binegar was selected back in the mid-60s as one of the stations used for the census to determine the viability of the line, and how grateful the people of the surrounding villages were that it was carried out during term time when the station is a busy place.

The time has just turned ten past six as we come to a halt just over a mile or so from the summit of the line. Binegar can be a cruel place in the depths of winter months with snow laying for days on the higher part of Mendip. I remember the severe winter of 1963 when the line was blocked for several days.

It began to snow on Boxing Day and by the turn of the year severe blizzards were sweeping southwest England.

Conditions continued to deteriorate, a view not shared if you were a child at the time, and on the 3rd of January the line succumbed, blocked by massive snowdrifts. With some trains at a standstill in various locations it took over three days to clear a single line through to Shepton Mallet.

As a child I often though why does it snow on the Mendip Hills in winter and not at Midsomer Norton or Radstock. Well, the answer is quite simple. The surrounding areas are less than 300 feet above sea level. Now air temperature is reduced by 1 degree for every 330 feet of elevation. Snow rarely falls if the temperature is above 2 degrees. With an ambient temperature of 4 degrees at 300 feet the temperature on the higher parts of Mendip will be less than 2 degrees, with precipitation falling as snow rather than rain, quite straightforward really.

The S&D station buildings remain much as they were in the mid-60s.

The buildings, including the signal box on the up platform, have survived intact in the main due to the splendid work of the Somerset & Dorset Railway Steam Heritage Trust based at Midsomer Norton.

Binegar is currently the southern terminus for the steam hauled passenger trains that run from Midsomer Norton on special weekends throughout the year. The infrastructure has grown to include a turntable the trust was able to salvage from Evercreech Junction. The trust aims to install a small turntable at Midsomer Norton in the future so the engines can turn to run right way on both journeys.

The station is a hive of activity on those special weekends. The trust is always looking for new members and any donations are always most welcome.

The sidings see little use these days with the quarry traffic concentrated close to Windsor Hill Tunnels.

No snow today though as the warm early evening sun highlights the delightful rural location of the station.

After a brief stop to allow just a few passengers to alight we head south towards the highest point on the line.

In just over a mile we traverse the summit, no significance to this achievement today other than it is the highest point on the line, 811 feet or so above sea level. Far different in the days of steam when the driver and fireman could take it relatively easy after the severe climb that began back at Radstock. Our train will also coast with ease for the next 8 miles or so to Evercreech Junction.

The unpopular decision was taken to close Masbury Halt after the review, perhaps a token closure. However, plans are afoot to restore its status as a halt with the Somerset & Dorset Steam Heritage Trust at the fore. Part of their plan is to extend their steam services as far as Masbury.

When the Somerset & Dorset built the extension from Evercreech to Bath over a hundred years ago they named the station at Maesbury, Masbury, and the spelling of the station name has remained ever since sharing a parallel with the Ffestiniog Railway in North Wales.

The station at Masbury was opened in 1874 but was downgraded to a halt in 1938. The preserved substantial station buildings belie its remote location acquiring just a fleeting glimpse as we speed past with the undulating Somerset countryside ahead of reaching Shepton Mallet.

Situated just north of the twin bores of Winsor Hill tunnels are the extensive sidings of the Hamwood and Winsor Hill quarries. Both continue to thrive with their easy access to the nations rail network.

SHEPTON MALLET

Descending steeply from the Mendip Hills we pass through Winsor Hill Tunnel, almost an unnoticed event for the passenger, just a momentary period of darkness. The same for today's driver, unlike his counterparts from the steam ere where the restrictive bore created an inferno on the footplate.

As we continue to sweep southwards, we cross the six arched 62 feet high Bath Road Viaduct

We then cross the longer twenty-seven arch viaduct built on a curve, ahead of reaching the station at Shepton Mallet.

The booking office and waiting rooms are still much as they were on the up platform with the signal box and original shelter still in place on the down platform.

The small goods yard is still in regular use, frequented by Clarks shoe factory and a nearby quarry.

The town's main employer, Showering, have their own dedicated siding in the goods yard.

Twice weekly a container train pulls away from the station laden with wagons destined for distribution through the British Isles and beyond.

Much of the raw materials used in the manufacture are also brought in by rail, alleviating the strain on the already congested roads.

Passenger number on the line have steadily grown over the years due to the residential development in the town, now commuters can catch the early morning train north to Bath, with journey times cut to under forty minutes.

The junction at Radstock now provides the option to travel to London Paddington. An alternative is to travel south to Evercreech Junction, connecting with the scheduled train to Bournemouth, changing at Templecombe for London Waterloo.

The station here can become a busy place at various times of the year. With its proximity to the popular Bath & West Show it becomes quite congested in late June.

Additional trains are laid on with passenger services arriving from Bournemouth, Bath and Bristol. A fleet of buses are used to transport people to and from the site a few miles away.

There is talk of, but whether anything will come of it, a siding constructed on the line near to Prestleigh Viaduct with a single platform to alleviate the situation.

The siding with new platform would be exclusively for showground use, a venue that now hosts several other major events during the year.

The Somerset & Dorset Steam Heritage Trust based at Midsomer Norton already have plans underway to reach Masbury in sight. However long-term aspirations by some see their goal as reaching Shepton Mallet.

What a scenic steam train experience that would be with the long relentless climb from Midsomer Norton up over the Mendip Hills, before coasting into Shepton Mallet across the two viaducts.

Looking further ahead they would see the way forward as negotiating to use the siding at Prestleigh, if that ambitious scheme were to get the go ahead.

The time is a quarter past six, so we must wait a short time before we continue south to Evercreech.

A good time to maybe take a moment to ponder the journey so far. It seems no time at all since we coasted from under the vaulted glass roof at Bath Green Park, pausing at Bath Junction, to complete a token exchange.

A short almost unnoticeable climb through to Midford before the tight twists and turns through the Wellow Valley. The industrial sidings continue to flourish at Radstock.

The junction is one of the most important stations on the line with the connection to Bristol and more so London Paddington, via Westbury.

The once relentless climb up over Mendip was taken with ease, the only poignant note, passing through Masbury, no longer a halt on the line. But we must be grateful that the railway has survived and is a very well used resource today.

Enough musing for now because at this point, we have the rest of the journey to look forward to.

As we ease away from the station the next noteworthy section is the run towards the increasingly famous viaduct at Prestleigh.

We are now nearing the end of our journey, but before we reach our destination at Evercreeh Junction we cross the impressive eleven arch stone viaduct close to the village of Prestleigh.

The graceful stone structure has become a celebrated tourist attraction thanks in no small way to featuring in a film version of a famous children's novel.

The viaduct was used as a location in the film and featured the Somerset & Dorset Steam locomotive steaming northwards over the viaduct.

Extra Mk1 maroon coaches were brought in to add authenticity to the scene with an impressive eleven coaches seen crossing the viaduct, hauled behind the trusts 9F 922207 Morning Star.

Visitors now arriving by road and rail bring much needed income for local businesses.

EVERCREECH

Easing into the station I see the sign for Evercreech. Even so we've not arrived at our intended destination just yet, as this is the station in the heart of the village, some two miles north of the Junction.

Running on time it's just before twenty past six, a mere forty minutes or so since we left Bath. Evercreech is at times a busy station with frequent movement from the sidings that serve a limestone works and the milk industry.

The buildings appear very neglected when compared to the pristine condition of Midsomer Norton, but there are no volunteers here to offer their services. The shelter on the up platform has been replaced with a rather modern version identical to the one installed at Chilcompton.

EVERCREECH JUNCTION

The junction here at Evercreech has existed since the proposal was put forward to extend the line northwards to Bath in 1874. The junction was the station for Evercreech on the original Somerset & Dorset line. A decision was taken to accommodate it on the new extension two miles north, a far more convenient site for the village.

We run in at low speed passing the branch off to the right to Burnham-on-Sea. This was the site of the turntable, now installed at Binegar for The Somerset & Dorset Steam Heritage Trust before being relocated, no longer required for the modern diesel engine.

The junction today is a very busy place. The long-established through trains direct from Bath to Bournemouth are a thing of the past with the service from Bath now terminating here at Evercreech Junction.

The onward journey south is continued at speed with a mirror image service, with trains running between Bournemouth Central and Evercreech Junction on a regular daily basis.

The timetable today ensures sufficient time, but no unnecessary long delay, to achieve the connection.

There are now six roads with two island platforms serving the junction. The stone buildings have been demolished to make way for a modern terminus. Trains from Bath arrive at Platform One and return to Bath from Platform Two. Platform Three is used by trains heading to Bournemouth with Platform Four receiving the arrival service. Platform Five and Six caters for the branch to Burnham-on-Sea with departures leaving from Platform Six.

The six roads are connected allowing for easy interchange.

The platforms are connected by series of subways. The main station buildings are located on the new island platform serving both the Bath and Bournemouth lines, housing the large booking office and comfortable waiting rooms.

Lesser waiting rooms are located on the other platforms.

The main buildings offer a large restaurant and separate refreshment room for a quick cup of tea to take on your journey.

A shop offers newspapers and stationery items.

The train comes to a halt on time at 18.22, far easier to achieve today than it would have been for the crew of a steam engine battling its way over the Mendip hills back in the days of steam.

Now it's all change as I'm on the way to Burnham-on-Sea, but I should have enough time to grab a bite to eat in the restaurant before my train leaves at five to seven.

Once off the train I use the subway to Platform Two where the main buildings are located. The substantial restaurant, aptly named The Somerset & Dorset, caters for a wide variety of tastes and is well frequented, even by non-rail users.

A generous area within is dedicated to The Somerset & Dorset Steam Heritage Trust, adorned with photographs and memories of the halcyon days of steam.

The displays are provided and looked after by the dedicated volunteers at Midsomer Norton.

A light snack and I head for Platform Six, picking up a late edition of the local evening newspaper on the way.

The onward journey to Burnham-on-Sea is in complete contrast to the line from Bath, relatively level with long stretches of straight track, no awkward contours to negotiate, indeed this was part of the original Somerset & Dorset Joint Railway before the Bath extension was envisaged.

My next train is standing at Platform Six having arrived at 18.32 from Burnham-on-Sea, establishing a vital connection with the service from Bath.

The junction is not just the preserve of the fare paying passenger.

To the north lie the six-road marshalling yard and extensive sidings. The easy access afforded by the railway has attracted a large influx of business to the area, bringing with it much needed prosperity.

OH! MR PORTER

My connecting train is now standing at Platform Six.

An announcement is made, " The train now standing on Platform Three is the 18.55 to Bournemouth Central, calling at Cole Halt, Wincanton, Templecombe South, Stalbridge Halt, Sturminster Newton, Shillingstone, Blanford Forum and Broadstone".

Today the journey south is far quicker than in 1966. The station that served the tiny village of Henstridge experienced the same fate as Masbury Halt.

Quite a lot of information there. In truth there are just a handful of people at the junction tonight now the 18.45 has departed for Bournemouth. Not so the case at certain times of year.

The summer months are busy with holiday makers arriving from the north to catch the connection to what is now Bournemouth Central, allowing ease of onward journeys to

Swanage and Weymouth. Bournemouth West was recommended for closure in the review.

The journey from Evercreech Junction to Bournemouth Central is completed in under an hour aided in no small way by relatively level terrain and with just a handful of stops.

The route south to the Dorset coast is very different to the journey embarked on from Bath.

The first station out of Evercreech Junction is Cole, originally named Cole for Bruton. Next, only four miles further on, is Wincanton where several significant changes have taken place. The station is always a very popular alighting place on race days, where specially chartered trains arrive from far and wide. An additional platform now helps to ease congestion.

The goods yard has been developed to cope with increased freight, including the large expansion of Cow & Gate, who now send heavily laden tanker wagons of milk to London via the rail network daily.

However, the most noteworthy change for passengers has taken place at Templecombe where the line reverts to single track working for the next 16 miles to Blanford Forum.

No longer do trains divert to run into Templecombe Station as they did in the days of steam, thus avoiding the laborious task of reversing back to the main line to continue the journey south. Just a short pause is all that is required at the token exchange point for the driver to requests the token for the section of single line ahead.

The original platform on the Somerset & Dorset line between a road bridge and a bridge carrying the Exeter to Waterloo Line was closed way before the review of the railways was published but has now been brought back into service. There is just a tiny booking office, and a small waiting room built into the hillside.

A pedestrian path from the platform now allows passengers to change to the main Exeter to Waterloo line a few hundred yards from the station.

The new station was named Templecombe South.

Continuing south the train passes swiftly through the tiny village of Henstridge, no longer stopping here, not even a request stop these days, although villagers are petitioning to restore its status as a halt.

The halt at Stalbridge is next before the station at Sturminster Newton. Several automatic level crossings have been installed along the route replacing the need for staff to man them.

The station at Shillingstone remains open ahead of Blanford Forum. Most stations on this the old Dorset part of the original joint railway thankfully remain intact. All appear in reasonably good condition. Many now enjoy listed building status, and rightfully so.

At Blanford Forum the token is given up as we enter double line working all the way into Bournemouth Central.

A bold decision had to be taken during the review to concentrate all traffic to one station, with the larger terminus at Bournemouth Central chosen as the most suitable location.

Initially met with some protest the plans for amalgamation were finally agreed on the basis that it was better to have a terminus there rather than no railway.

The line to Burnham-on-Sea is busy but not to the same degree, save for late June. For a few days every year the station is an unendurable place to pass through.

Picture a scene if you can with up to three trains arriving within minutes. All are jam packed full of revellers all intent on heading west, and crammed onto platform six, their destination West Pennard Halt.

The temporary halt becomes alive at that time of year, the dropping off point closest to Worthy Farm at Pilton for the annual pop festival. Officially as many as 35,000 people descend on Worthy Farm, each paying up to £13 for the weekend spectacular.

They say the aim is to grow the festival year by year attracting ever larger crowds, imagine the effect on the infrastructure if the crowds were ever to reach 100,000.

No such congestion tonight. Almost time to set off and plenty of seats to choose from. Now a while since I made this journey and I think the best views will open up if I sit on the left side of the carriage.

An effortless passage away from the station soon finds the train back in open countryside heading for Burnham-on-Sea.

PYLLE HALT

Pylle Halt as it is known is located on the Fosse Way and is a popular station with commuters. There is easy parking for those not wishing to travel into Shepton Mallet. Throughout the day the station is a tranquil place, apart that is from the noise of traffic using the notorious A37 Shepton Mallet to Ilchester Road.

With its position under two miles from Evercreech Junction the sidings are no longer in use, all freight has been diverted to the nearby goods yard at the junction.

Just the modern-day shelters can be seen on the platforms having replaced the original stone buildings.

The old station masters house and goods shed along with the single box have been demolished. This single line is temporarily doubled through the station creating a passing loop allowing the token exchange to take place.

No one alighting or boarding our train this evening, so we pass slowly through the station without stopping.

In stark contrast to the tight twists and turns encountered on the Bath extension we descend on a 1 in 86 gradient Roman road fashion, heading west toward Glastonbury.

WEST PENNARD HALT

The transient halt at West Pennard is soon upon us as we reach the foot of the four-mile incline from Pylle Halt.

With the location of the station some two miles from the village it was inevitable that it would fall foul of the review.

The station building has long gone but two bare platforms remain and once a year the station is rejuvenated, gaining its status for just a few days to serve the nearby Pop Festival at Pilton, or Glastonbury Festival as it is being increasingly called.

In complete contrast to the calm of tonight the place resembles a beehive during late June. A throng of festival goers arrive hourly for two days with the whole process reversed just a few days later, alas now and again in a muddy situation.

No such festival tonight so we steam past, if that is the right term to use in these days of the diesel.

Continuing directly ahead we approach the Somerset Levels.

I certainly made the right choice sitting on the left, taking in the magnificent views of Glastonbury Tor. We head ever closer to the town by the second as we speed along the level track bed.

GLASTONBURY

The approach to the station passes the old junction for Wells. The branch was closed in 1951 due in part the city was served by the line from Witham Friary.

Glastonbury has now become a busy tourist attraction with its abbey ruins at the centre. The town abounds in mystic and mystery, fuelled no doubt by the tor and the legends that flourish. However, just one name sums up Glastonbury and its near neighbour Street, and that is of course Clarks.

Clarks shoes have been well established in Street since 1825. Brothers James and Cyrus made their first pair of slippers from the off cuts in the tannery which they were working. The company rapidly grew and in the late 1940s the workforce in Street were unable to cope with demand.

When a decision was made to open several new factories in the neighbouring towns, Bath, Radstock (Westfield) and Shepton Mallet we chosen.

All seen as suitable locations with the railways allowing fluent distribution of essential raw materials.

The finished products are returned by rail back to Street for onward transportation through the rail system. Clarks now boast a modern dedicated distribution centre located within the extensive goods yard at the station in Glastonbury.

The station at Glastonbury was once named Glastonbury and Street reflecting its proximity with its neighbour but was shortened to just Glastonbury during modernisation.

The large station has been downsized and the original wooden building with their generous canopies replaced with a modern equivalent housing a booking hall, waiting rooms and a small buffet.

The island platform that jointly served the Wells Branch and the Burnham-on Sea line now houses just the standard modern-day shelter.

Only a brief stop at Glastonbury to allow just a handful of passengers to alight. The radio token exchange system is again in use covering the next controlled section of single track.

The line running from Evercreech Junction to Burnham-on-Sea was built as single track when it first operated as the Somerset & Dorset Joint Railway. Owing to the limited service doubling of the track has never been a feasible option.

The motion is almost undetectable moving gradually away from the platform we drift with ease along the level track, now almost at sea level and as the crow flies.

As well as the stark comparison to the Bath extension with its tight curves and steep gradients the line has a scattering of minor level crossings. These were once operated from crossing keepers' cottages, but all are now fully automated.

During the golden age of steam there were four small stations along the twelve mile stretch of track from Glastonbury to Highbridge, just one remains at Shapwick, downgraded to a halt.

The Somerset levels roll by with very little movement felt in the carriage as the train continues to pass effortlessly along the track.

As we near Shapwick Halt it soon becomes apparent why a station and goods yard have been retained, passing as we do vast fields of peat.

Peat has been harvested from the Somerset Levels as far back as Roman times. Production seems to be declining but the goods yard can be a busy place at certain times of the year.

SHAPWICK HALT

Situated as it is some two miles from the village it is no small wonder the halt sees very little use, aside from a few commuters. Just two bare platforms affording no shelter and a passing loop is the best way to describe this rural halt.

The adjacent goods yard, now given over entirely to peat industry is in a rather neglected condition, overgrown in places by annual weeds.

One point of distinction was the 1963 John Betjeman BBC programme, "Branch Line Railway", featuring the line and Shapwick Station.

Our train slows briefly but soon regains its momentum as it becomes apparent that no one needs the service at Shapwick tonight.

We continue at good pace passing in the blink of an eye the site of Edington Junction. The junction was once a busy place where the line branched off to Bridgwater. Closed in 1954 all that remains today is our single track.

We are soon passing through Bason Bridge, an exceptional setting on the line as there is no passenger facility, the station only serving the significant goods yard.

Located close to Highbridge a decision was made to close the station to passenger traffic as it was considered superfluous during the review. The sidings are at the present time used by the United Dairies Milk Company and several other businesses including the cider industry, due in the main to exceptional road and rail links.

HIGHBRIDGE

Sitting all alone in the carriage my mind begins to wander back to the days of steam and eventually my thoughts drift to travel times and how they have been reduced.

Now I picked up a summer timetable at Bath, what on earth have I done with that. Must have left it behind at Evercreech when I had a bite to eat. Unnervingly there's also no trace of a late edition evening newspaper I bought back at the station.

However, my immediate attention is soon diverted back to the present time as the scenery transforms approaching Highbridge.

We leave behind the rural idyll for the first time, apart that is from brief interludes at Radstock, Midsomer Norton and Shepton Mallet since leaving Bath.

We pass row after row of goods sheds and heavily laden wagons in the large, regenerated marshalling yard connected to the distant Highbrige Wharf.

Industrial cranes dominate the landscape to the south.

We are still running on single track in complete contrast to the numerous sidings adjacent. The yard is home to a substantial sawmill and a large fuel depot, as well as catering for numerous other industrial demands.

The approach to the station is slow as we run over countless points passing vast piles of coal and countless buildings, one housing a vast wagon works. The old engine sheds now diversified from their creative purpose back in the age of steam.

The original turntable is still in place, used very occasionally for chartered steam services run by British Rail.

There are five platforms at Highbridge Station although today only two are used for passenger services. No modern building at Highbridge, the traditional stone ones have been refurbished to cater for modern day needs.

Just a few yards from where we have come to a halt is the main Taunton to Bristol line. Two footbridges allow passenger to change services from the station.

Highbridge is now a true commuter station in the sense of the word and serves daily the many industrial sites adjacent to the railway.

The station provides an essential connection from Evercreech junction, with passengers able to change for Bristol and perhaps more significantly a direct line to the county town of Taunton.

We are soon underway on the short stretch of line to journeys end at Burnham-on-Sea, crossing over the busy intersection on the way.

BURNHAM-ON-SEA

An awe-inspiring sunset now greets us as we near journeys end on the Somerset Coast. The bustling resort of Burnham-On-Sea has prospered helped in no small way by station remaining open.

Throughout summer several excursions are added to the timetable bringing thousands of extra visitors, some come for the day others stay a week.

The Pontins Holiday camp was taken over by Butlins and is now one of their flagship resorts, providing high levels of employment for the surrounding areas. The high Street has seen a boom with outlets for most of the major retailers now trading in the town, again boosted by the arrival of seasonal visitors.

As we coast into the station the sea comes into view, glistening this evening as the sun sets over Exmoor away in the far distance.

The terminus at Burnham underwent extensive refurbishment shortly after the review, now boasting four roads served by a large island platform and two either side.

One platform continues beyond the main island platform to serve as additional sidings for special excursions.

At the far end of the island platform is the large booking office and waiting room. A sizeable restaurant has been built alongside and is a popular destination for both rail and non-rail users. A tourist information centre and a small newsagents serve both rail passengers and foot visitors alike.

During the very busy summer season at weekends up to six extra trains a day can arrive in Burnham-on-Sea. The scheduling must be spot on to allow free movement over the entire single line working through to Evercreech Junction.

There is a small goods yard, seldom used today as local freight is best served by the extensive sidings back at Highbridge. Had the carriage all to myself since we left the station at Glastonbury. Best get ready to get off although the strange thing is I'm not sure why I've come to Burnham-on-Sea tonight.

I find myself frantically searching through my pockets for a rail ticket. Thinking out loud I am asking what have I done with it, where could I have put it? I begin to feel sweat on my brow but can't find the damn thing anywhere. All I come across are a few notes and oddly a pay and display car park receipt.

Curious thing is the same fate befell a chap in the next seat to me when we arrived at his destination back in Glastonbury. I bought a ticket back at Bath Green Park, I'm certain that I did.

I check through my wallet but find no trace of any ticket, the only thing relative to the railways is a card telling me I am a member of The Somerset & Dorset Railway Heritage Trust.

We continue at a snail's pace approaching the end of the line. The place seems eerily deserted tonight, even the restaurant that I know is habitually packed is unexpectedly quiet.

There is a surreal aura at the station tonight, even the sunset that greeted our train seems to be fading rapidly and turning hazy.

JUST LIKE MY DREAMS

The train inexplicably comes to an abrupt halt. There is a sudden jolt and in next to no time it soon becomes evident that all I have witnessed on my journey doesn't exist, swept away by the merciless actions of a few. There is no ticket! there never was.

My watch confirms the time as 18.40. I recall leaving Bath Green Park at 17.42 on my journey home to Chilcompton, I should have arrived there by now.

Wiping the sweat from my furrowed brow I soon grasp that the journey has been a dream, not a nightmare as the perspiration is due to the humid atmosphere in my stationery car.

The nightmare is here right now, sat going nowhere in a colossal traffic jam on the A367 north of Radstock. Looking down towards the town I see no sign of any railway station.

I enquire of a gentleman passing what the issue is this evening. He responds in a gruff tone. *"There's a tree down there blocking the road."*

He continues rather crotchety. *"Don't worry mate I've got an axe, a bloody big one, so I can easily remove it"*. I asked if he was called Beeching, but he never replied, he just continued towards Radstock muttering vociferously to himself and swinging his axe as he went.

What if there had been an announcer back at Bath Green Park. More significantly what if there had been no Beeching et al.

Just like my dreams..................

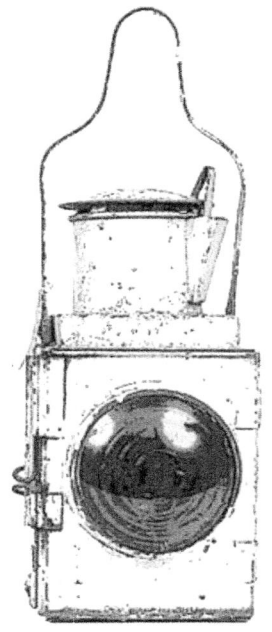

Printed in Dunstable, United Kingdom